First World War
and Army of Occupation
War Diary
France, Belgium and Germany

1 INDIAN CAVALRY DIVISION
Divisional Troops
Divisional Signal Squadron
28 December 1914 - 31 December 1916

WO95/1170/6

The Naval & Military Press Ltd
www.nmarchive.com
Published in association with The National Archives

Published by

The Naval & Military Press Ltd

Unit 10 Ridgewood Industrial Park,

Uckfield, East Sussex,

TN22 5QE England

Tel: +44 (0) 1825 749494

www.naval-military-press.com

www.nmarchive.com

This diary has been reprinted in facsimile from the original. Any imperfections are inevitably reproduced and the quality may fall short of modern type and cartographic standards.

© **Crown Copyright**
Images reproduced by permission of The National Archives, London, England, 2015.

Contents

Document type	Place/Title	Date From	Date To
Heading	WO95/1170/6		
Heading	BEF 1 Ind. Cav. Div. Troops Signal Sqd 1914 Dec To 1916 Dec		
Heading	War Diary of Signal Squadron 1st Indian Cavalry Division. From 28th December 1914 To 28th February 1915		
War Diary	Field	28/12/1914	28/02/1915
Heading	War Diary of Signal Squadron 1st Indian Cavalry Division From 1st March 1915 30th April 1915.		
War Diary	Inclusive Norrent-Fontes.	01/03/1915	06/03/1915
War Diary	Norrent Fontes	07/03/1915	11/03/1915
War Diary	At Marles	11/03/1915	15/03/1915
War Diary	At Bourecq	16/03/1915	28/04/1915
Heading	War Diary of Signal Squadron, 1st Indian Cavalry Division. From 1st May 1915 To 30th June 1915.		
War Diary		01/05/1915	30/06/1915
Heading	War Diary of Signal Squadron, 1st Indian Cavalry Division. From 1st July 1915 To 31st August 1915		
War Diary		01/07/1915	03/09/1915
War Diary		02/08/1915	03/08/1915
Heading	War Diary of Signal Squadron, 1st Indian Cavalry Division From 1st September, 1915 To 30th September 1915		
War Diary		01/09/1915	30/09/1915
Heading	War Diary with Appendices of Signal Squadron, 1st Indian Cavalry Division From 1st October 1915 To 31st October 1915		
War Diary	Le Meillard	01/10/1915	07/10/1915
War Diary	Domart	13/10/1915	13/10/1915
War Diary	Lequesnoy	22/10/1915	31/10/1915
Diagram etc	Communications 1st Ind. Cav. Div. 2nd Nov 1915		
Heading	War Diary of Signal Squadron, 1st Indian Cavalry Division From 1st November 1915 To 31st December 1915		
War Diary	Le Quesnoy	01/11/1915	15/12/1915
War Diary	Dargnies.	16/12/1915	31/12/1915
Diagram etc	Communications. V.I.A. 24.XII.15		
Heading	War Diary of Signal Squadron 1st. Indian Cavalry Division From 1st January 1916 To 31st January 1916		
War Diary	Dargnies	01/01/1916	31/01/1916
Heading	War Diary of Signal Squadron, 1st Indian Cavalry Division From 1st February 1916 To 29th February 1916		
War Diary	Dargnies	01/02/1916	29/02/1916
Heading	War Diary of Signal Squadron, 1st Indian Cavalry Division From 1st March 1916 To 31st March 1916		
War Diary	Dargnies	05/03/1916	31/03/1916
Heading	War Diary of Signal Squadron, 1st Indian Cavalry Division From 1st April 1916 To 30th April 1916		
War Diary	Wail	01/04/1916	23/04/1916

Heading	War Diary of Signal Squadron, 1st Indian Cavalry Division From 1st May 1916 To 30th June 1916		
War Diary	Yvrench	01/05/1916	06/05/1916
War Diary	Wail	07/05/1916	07/05/1916
War Diary	Le Cauroy	10/05/1916	30/06/1916
Heading	War Diary of Signal Squadron, 1st Indian Cavalry Division From 1st July 1916 To 31st July 1916		
War Diary	Doullens	02/07/1916	02/07/1916
War Diary	Auxi Le Chateau	03/07/1916	13/07/1916
War Diary	Villers Chatel	19/07/1916	31/07/1916
Heading	War Diary of Signal Squadron, 1st Indian Cavalry Division From 1st August 1916 To 31st August 1916		
War Diary	Villers Chatel	09/08/1916	31/08/1916
Heading	War Diary of Signal Squadron, 1st Indian Cavalry Division From 1st September 1916 To 30th September 1916		
War Diary	Frohen Legrand	02/09/1916	04/09/1916
War Diary	Doullens	11/09/1916	11/09/1916
War Diary	Allonville	13/09/1916	13/09/1916
War Diary	Morlancourt	15/09/1916	23/09/1916
War Diary	Montauban	25/09/1916	25/09/1916
War Diary	Morlancourt	25/09/1916	26/09/1916
War Diary	Bussy Les Daours	27/09/1916	27/09/1916
War Diary	Picquigny	28/09/1916	28/09/1916
War Diary	Ailly Le Haut Clocher	29/09/1916	29/09/1916
War Diary	Ligescourt	30/09/1916	30/09/1916
Heading	War Diary of Signal Squadron, 4th Cavalry Division (late 1st Ind. Cavy. Divn). From 1st October 1916 To 30th November 1916		
War Diary	Ligescourt	01/10/1916	10/11/1916
War Diary	St Valery	11/11/1916	30/11/1916
Heading	War Diary of Signal Squadron, 4th Cavalry Division From 1st December 1916 To 31st December 1916		
War Diary	St Valery	01/12/1916	31/12/1916
Diagram etc	Communications VD 12.12.16		
Heading	###		
Heading	War Diary of Head Quarters R.A. 1st Indian Cavalry Division From 7th April 1915 To 28th May. 1915.		
Heading	War Diary of Hd Qrs RA 1st Indian Cavalry Division April May 1915		
Heading	War Diary of Hd Qrs R.A. 1st Indian Cavalry Division March-1915.		
Heading	War Diary of Hd Qrs R.A. 1st Indian Cavalry Division February-1915		

No 95/1170/9

BEF

1 IND. CAV. DIV. TROOPS

SIGNAL SQD

1914 Dec - 1916 DEC

Serial No. 145

WAR DIARY

Signal Squadron: 1st Indian Cavalry Division.

From 28th December 1914 to 28th February 1915

Original

Army Form C. 2118.

WAR DIARY of Signal Squadron 1st Ind. Cav. Div

or

INTELLIGENCE SUMMARY.

(Erase heading not required.)

Instructions regarding War Diaries and Intelligence Summaries are contained in F. S. Regs., Part II. and the Staff Manual respectively. Title pages will be prepared in manuscript.

Hour, Date, Place.	Summary of Events and Information	Remarks and references to Appendices.
Field		
Dec 28th 1914	Squadron formed at NORRENT FONTES under command of Capt. H. Evans R.E. Communication opened with 2nd Cav" Corps and Brigades. R. & O. 11th Hussars Lt. L. Borthwick - joined - 2nd Officer not yet appointed	
Dec 29th to 31st	A joined - Squadron remained at NORRENT FONTES Nothing to report - Squadron remained at NORRENT FONTES	
Jan 1st 1915 - Jan 16	" " " " " " " "	
Jan 17th	Lt. R. L. Atkinson 17th Cavalry joined.	
Jan 22nd	Field exercise - Divisional.	
Jan 29	" " "	
Feb 4	" "	
Feb 16th	Major H. Evans R.E. proceeded home to report to War Office Lt. Borthwick assumes Command.	
	" " granted temp" rank of Capt. while in Command	
Feb 23rd	Signal Squadron Field exercise - Divisional	

Army Form C. 2118.

Original

WAR DIARY

or of Signal Squadron

INTELLIGENCE SUMMARY.

1st The Cavly Sqn.

(Erase heading not required.)

Instructions regarding War Diaries and Intelligence Summaries are contained in F. S. Regs., Part II, and the Staff Manual respectively. Title pages will be prepared in manuscript.

Hour, Date, Place.	Summary of Events and Information	Remarks and references to Appendices.
Field Feb 27th.	Lt. A. H. A. Emerson 8th Cavalry joined Signal Squadron from Corps Signal Squadron.	
Feb 28th.	Squadron still in billets at NORRENT FONTES. Average of messages sent and received daily about 250. for period Jan 1st to Feb 28th. Average of messages sent or received by telegraph or telephone about 83.	

L. Brook-Hank Capt
Cmdg
Signal Squadron
1st Indian Cavalry Division

Serial No. 145

121/5504

WAR DIARY

OF

Signal Squadron, 1st Indian Cavalry Division.

From 1st March 1915 to 30th April 1915.

Army Form C. 2118.

Signal Squadron
1st I.D. Cav Bgde

WAR DIARY
or
INTELLIGENCE SUMMARY

(Erase heading not required.)

Instructions regarding War Diaries and Intelligence Summaries are contained in F. S. Regs., Part II. and the Staff Manual respectively. Title pages will be prepared in manuscript.

Hour, Date, Place.	Summary of Events and Information	Remarks and references to Appendices.
March 1st – 6th inclusive NORRENT – FONTES.	Division in same billeting area as previous month.	All maps annotated forwarded to Squadron HQ Cav Corps.
March 7th NORRENT FONTES	Division moved up to close billetings	
March 11th March 12, 13, 14 at MARLES	Squads to MARLES. Forces report centre MARLES 5 H am back report centre close 7 am NORRENT FONTES	
March 15th March 16, 17 at BOURECQ	Moved back to BOURECQ – spells 5.30 am Head-	
March 18th	Division moved to ENQUIN area. HQ at ENQUIN	
March 19th to April 23rd	At ENQUIN – in the three hours notice to move.	
April 24th	Division ordered to move. Moved depart Scheme issued ST MARIE CAPPEL at 6 pm – close ENQUIN next issue	
April 25th & 27th	At ST MARIE CAPPEL	

Army Form C. 2118.

WAR DIARY
or
INTELLIGENCE SUMMARY.
(Erase heading not required.)

Instructions regarding War Diaries and Intelligence Summaries are contained in F. S. Regs., Part II, and the Staff Manual respectively. Title pages will be prepared in manuscript.

Hour, Date, Place.	Summary of Events and Information	Remarks and references to Appendices.
April 24th	Division ordered to move forward upto certain opera to ST MARIE CAPPEL at 6 p.m. CRO ENQUIN same time.	All major communication forwarded to Signal Sub Cav Corps
April 25th & 27th	At ST MARIE CAPPEL.	
April 28th	Division moved to WATOU. speed there at mid-day	
April 29th to 30th inclusive	At WATOU	
		Capt. [signature] Brookes Anst Signal Troop 1st Ind Cav Div

Serial No. 145.

12/6/28

WAR DIARY

OF

Signal Squadron, 1st Indian Cavalry Division.

From 1st May 1915. To 30th June 1915.

Army Form C. 2118

WAR DIARY
or
INTELLIGENCE SUMMARY.
Of Signal Squadron
1st Ind. Cav. Div.

(Erase heading not required.)

Instructions regarding War Diaries and Intelligence Summaries are contained in F. S. Regs., Part II, and the Staff Manual respectively. Title pages will be prepared in manuscript.

Hour, Date, Place.	Summary of Events and Information	Remarks and references to Appendices.
May 1st 1915	Divisional HQ at WATOU. No cable laid - all communication by DR.	All maps were forwarded to Regs YCO
May 2nd 1915	Moved back to St. Marie Cappel. Comm's still by DR.	
" 3rd - 4th	At St. Marie Cappel.	
" 5th	Moved to ROQUETOIRE area. HQ in ROQUETOIRE. Laid cable to all Bdes	
" 6th - 16th inclusive	At ROQUETOIRE. No event of an importance.	
" 17th	Division moved - HQ to ALLOUAGNE. Comm'n by DR	
" 18th	At ALLOUAGNE.	
" 19th	Returned ROQUETOIRE area.	
" 27th	Moved to STAPLE (HQ). Division under orders of 2nd Army	
" 28th	"B" echelon also moved to RUBROUCK - waiting horse set- to gd. Army HQ. Fighting troops and towards Poperinghe centre moved to RENINGHELST and VLAMERTINGHE area. HQ at RENINGHELST. In direct comm'n by Telephone	

Army Form C. 2118
(2)

WAR DIARY
or
INTELLIGENCE SUMMARY.   Signal Regt.
(Erase heading not required.)

Hour, Date, Place.	Summary of Events and Information	Remarks and references to Appendices.
May 28th 1915	And telegraph with Fifth Corps. — By D.R. to Bdes. dbl cable to 15 Bde - comm: opened by P. lines.	
" 29th "	Division in same places.	
" 30th to June 2nd inclusive		
June 3rd	Jackson Bde. ordered in support of 3rd Cav. Div. to HOOGE excl. Comm: with them via line laid direct to 3rd Cav. Div. HQ at "GOLD FISH" CHâteau 1 mile W. of YPRES.	
June 4th	as for 3rd.	
June 5th	Jackson Bde. returned to Division	
June 6th – 10th inclusive	No change.	
June 11th	HQ of Division moved to POPERINGHE. Came on to front line to 5th Corps - made use of a permanent railway route line for Bdes. Picked up old KEMMINGHELST line to Bdes.	
June 15th	Sixth Corps laid line direct to Signal Office for "Ypres" messages.	

Gulab Singh & Sons, Calcutta—No. 22 Army C.—5-8-14—1,07,000.

WAR DIARY
or
INTELLIGENCE SUMMARY. Signal Squadron
(Erase heading not required.) 1st I.C.D.

Army Form C. 2118

June (3)

Instructions regarding War Diaries and Intelligence Summaries are contained in F. S. Regs., Part II, and the Staff Manual respectively. Title pages will be prepared in manuscript.

Hour, Date, Place.	Summary of Events and Information	Remarks and references to Appendices.
June 13th 1918 - June 14th	Same places as previous day.	
	Howard's report circuits rejoined "B" echelon at RUBROUCK. Average of daily messages at 1st Bde 223. Priority messages Ratio 1 in 7. Area 1 in 9. 6th Bde about 1 in 14 at F.R.C.	
June 15th	Division returned to consolidated ROQUETOIRE area. Cable laid to "B" Bde.	
June 16th - June 30th	At Roquetoire - no details	

E. Brook Lieut Colonel
Signal Squadron
1st Ind Cav Div.

Serial No. 145.

12/6948

WAR DIARY
OF

Signal Squadron, 1st Indian Cavalry Division.

FROM 1st July 1915 TO 31st August 1915

Army Form C. 2118.

WAR DIARY of Signal Squadron 1st Ind Cav Divn

INTELLIGENCE SUMMARY.

(Erase heading not required.)

Instructions regarding War Diaries and Intelligence Summaries are contained in F. S. Regs., Part II, and the Staff Manual respectively. Title pages will be prepared in manuscript.

Hour, Date, Place.	Summary of Events and Information	Remarks and references to Appendices.
July 1st 1915 to July 11th	At Roquetoire - In same billets, no change in communications from last period.	
" 12th		
" 13th	Air line erected to Dubola Cav Bde at Thiennes D. Head; through Sialkot Cav Bde at Blaringhem Chateau	Copy of communication forwarded to Sig: 1st Ind Cav Corps
" 14th	Air line erected to Lucknow Cav Bde at MAMETZ. One Officer & one N.C.O. attended from each Bde Troop for instruction.	
" 15th to 31st	At Roquetoire - Same billets, no change in communication.	

W. S. Waugh
Capt Commanding
Signal Squadron
1st Ind Cav Divn

WAR DIARY
INTELLIGENCE SUMMARY

of Signal Squadron — 1st Ind. Cav. Div —

Army Form C. 2118.

Hour, Date, Place.	Summary of Events and Information	Remarks and references to Appendices.
Aug 1st	Lt Rogerton — in curve billets Brigades started men to new billeting area communication by D.R.	Stagnum of communication attention to I.C.C.
Aug 2nd	Div H.Q. & signal squadron to ROYON	
Aug 3rd	" " " " — DOMART —	
Aug 4th	Laying cable to Aubvia Bde — Sialkote —	
" 5"	" " " " —	
5th — 18th	in telephonic communication with Lucknow Bde. on P.O. wire — Laying air lines picking up cable — all completed to the 3 Brigade. Routine work.	
18th — 22nd		
22nd	Advanced report centre move up to Marteusart in communication with 51st Div Brigades in trenches — 3rd Army. + I.C.C.	
2nd 3rd	Advd. report centre returned to billets left myself advd. report centre at MONTIGNY with digging parties —	WMayr — Capt. O.C. Sig. Sqdn. 1st Ind. Cav. Div

Serial No. 145

121/7286

WAR DIARY
OF

Signal Squadron, 1st Indian Cavalry Division.

From 1st September 1915 TO 30th September 1915

Army Form C. 2118.

WAR DIARY

of A Signal Squadron 1st Ind. Cav. Div.

INTELLIGENCE SUMMARY.

(Erase heading not required.)

Hour, Date, Place.	Summary of Events and Information	Remarks and references to Appendices.
Sept 1st – 22nd Sept	In Wecis in Domart in communication (metallic circuit) with all brigades	
22nd – 30th	Division moved to le Meillard in communication with all brigades by D.R.	

Warner Capt.
O.C. A Signal Squadron
1st Ind. Cav. Div.

121/7601

Serial No. 145

Confidential

War Diary

with Appendices

of

Signal Squadron, 1st Indian Cavalry Division

FROM 1st October 1915 TO 31st October 1915

Army Form C. 2118.

WAR DIARY
or
INTELLIGENCE SUMMARY.
(Erase heading not required.)

Signal Squadron
1st Ind. Cav. Div.

Instructions regarding War Diaries and Intelligence Summaries are contained in F. S. Regs., Part II, and the Staff Manual respectively. Title pages will be prepared in manuscript.

Hour, Date, Place.	Summary of Events and Information	Remarks and references to Appendices.
1st Oct 1915 — LE MEILLARD.		
7th Oct — "	Wireless circuit finished from Corps H.Q. to Div.	
13th Oct. DOMART —	Division H.Q. to lieu at DOMART. The communication with Corps H.Q. through the civil exchange. Communicate with brigades thru civil exchange by existing wires. All communications by D.R.	
OCT 22 LEQUESNOY.	Line laid to Corps H.Q. at WACCENCOURT.	
" 23 "	Telephone communication with Lucknow Bde.	
" 26 "	R.H.A. Bde H.Q. & ADMS, & ADVS	
" 30 "	Communication opened with Sialkote, MHOW	
" 31 "	Brigades — Field Squadron	
	All Regiments in communication with their Brigades by telephone —	Diagram of communications submitted

Viewto Bang — Capt.
O.C. Sig Sqdn 1st I.C.D.
1st Nov 1915

Communications 2nd Cav. Div. 2nd Nov 1915

- Gen Staff
- Q Staff
- GOC 1st Mess
- Sigs Mess

Diagram nodes/labels:
- I.C. (1st Cavalry)
- Le Quesnoy
- 1st C.C.D.
- Sialkote Bde
- Mhow Bde
- Lucknow Bde
- 17th Lancers Hangest
- 29th Lancers
- 19th Lancers
- 6th Cavalry
- 2nd Lancers
- Inniskilling Dragoons
- KDGs
- RHA Brigade
- ADMS
- ADVS
- Staff
- C.H.
- Field Squadron
- 36th J.H.

SERIAL NO. 145.

Confidential

War Diary

of

Signal Squadron, 1st Indian Cavalry Division.

FROM 1st November 1915 TO 31st December 1915.

Army Form C. 2118.

WAR DIARY
or
INTELLIGENCE SUMMARY. Signal Sqdn
1st Ind Cav Div

(Erase heading not required.)

Instructions regarding War Diaries and Intelligence Summaries are contained in F. S. Regs., Part II, and the Staff Manual respectively. Title pages will be prepared in manuscript.

Hour, Date, Place.	Summary of Events and Information	Remarks and references to Appendices.
Nov 1st LE QUESNOY	All brigades and regts in telephonic cme. Billets	CK 684 2/11/16
Nov 2nd "	Billets — routine work	
" 3rd "	Billets — Communication with Field Squadron at LISMER established	
" 4th–18th "	Billets All cme good	
" 19th "	Lucknow B.C. moved from CAPILLON to VIEULAINE — cme with them by DR	Diagram of communication submitted
" 20–23rd "	RHA headquarters moved to CROQUOISON — cme by DR Billets	
" 24th "	Air line to Lucknow B.C. completed — Billets	
" 25–27th "	Air line to RHA headquarters completed — Billets	Diagram of communication submitted
" 28, 29th "	Billets	
" 30th "	Capt Barge left to 9th Division. Lieut Erskine assumed Command. Billets	Messages this month maximum day 383 minimum 211 total 9037

A/H Erskine Lt
Comdg Signal Squadron 1st Ind Cav Div

Army Form C. 2118.

WAR DIARY
or
INTELLIGENCE SUMMARY. Signal Sqdn
1st I.C.D
(Erase heading not required.)

Instructions regarding War Diaries and Intelligence Summaries are contained in F. S. Regs., Part II, and the Staff Manual respectively. Title pages will be prepared in manuscript.

Hour, Date, Place.	Summary of Events and Information	Remarks and references to Appendices.
1st Dec. LE QUESNOY	Billets: line laid to U Battery	
2nd " "	" Communication all good	
3rd–9th "	"	
10th "	" "U" Battery line picked up	
14th "	Chateau and C. mess lines picked up. Captain R.H. Normanley-Smith, 14th Lancers, assumed command	
15th "	A.S.C., Q., Sig. Mess lines have been picked up	

A.M. Simpson N.

Army Form C. 2118.

WAR DIARY
or
INTELLIGENCE SUMMARY.

(Erase heading not required.)

Instructions regarding War Diaries and Intelligence Summaries are contained in F. S. Regs., Part II, and the Staff Manual respectively. Title pages will be prepared in manuscript.

Hour, Date, Place.	Summary of Events and Information	Remarks and references to Appendices.
16/12/15 Dargnies.	Marched from Dargnies from LEQUESNOY (via) & Telegraphic communication with y.Co.	
17/12/15 "	& Telegraphic communication with PIE (SANCOURT) Telephones hung up to G.O'Cs stations, GS & Q Officers, Sgn mess.	
18/12/15 "	On Telegraphic communication with P1H (FRANLEU) & Supply Column (BOUVAINCOURT) Billets - men get an easy day.	
19/12/15 "	Improving existing communications on line from VIA to P.I.B. collecting cable	
20/12/15 "	air line poles from old area. Owing to Bde. to departing at 8 am & 2 pm from 21/12/15 will further instructions the daily Reports will now run from 8.30 am to 8.30 am	
21/12/15 "	their preceding afternoon never before being transferred from one report to another during 21/12/15 in consequence return 22/12/15 up to 8.30 am EMBREUILLE	

Army Form C. 2118.

WAR DIARY
or
INTELLIGENCE SUMMARY.
(Erase heading not required.)

Instructions regarding War Diaries and Intelligence Summaries are contained in F. S. Regs., Part II, and the Staff Manual respectively. Title pages will be prepared in manuscript.

Hour, Date, Place.	Summary of Events and Information	Remarks and references to Appendices.
2+23/12/15 Morgnies	Lewis improvers toP/B - ordnance being not obtainable for cold.	
24/12/15 Dargnies	Lewis guns upto R.a Beauchamp. C.O.O.a formerly used by G. Co lent to class	
25th December DARGNIES	Billets. No turn out for xmas	
26" "	"	
27" "	"	
28" "	"	
29" "	" Heavy wind	
30" "	" Heavy wind	
31" "	" Heavy wind	

Messing for the month total 9348 maximum 400 minimum 160

R. M. Hammersley Lieut
Capt, 3/Res

Communications. V.I.A. 24 XII 15 -

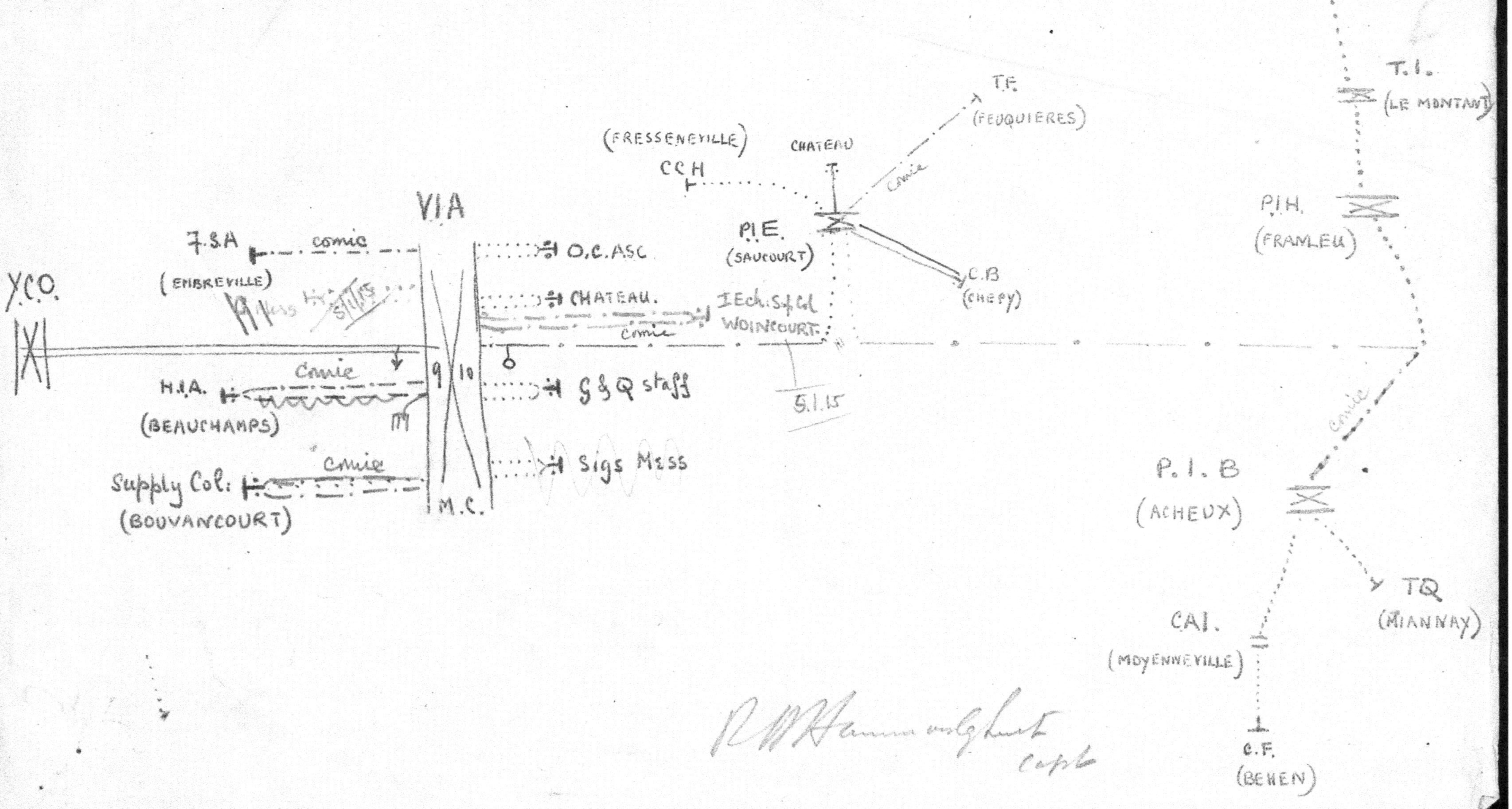
Y.C.O.
VIA
7.S.A
(EMBREVILLE)
comic
H.I.A.
(BEAUCHAMPS)
Comic
Supply Col:
(BOUVANCOURT)
Comic
9
10
M.C.
O.C. ASC
CHATEAU.
Comic
G & Q staff
Sigs Mess
I Ech. S. & Col
WOINCOURT.
5.1.15
(FRESSENEVILLE)
CCH
CHATEAU
P.I.E.
(SAUCOURT)
T.F.
(FEUQUIERES)
Comic
C.B
(CHEPY)
(SAIGNEVILLE)
C.B.I.
T.I.
(LE MONTANT)
P.I.H.
(FRAMLEU)
Comic
P.I.B
(ACHEUX)
TQ
(MIANNAY)
CAI.
(MOYENNEVILLE)
C.F.
(BEHEN)

Capt

SERIAL NO. 145.

Confidential

War Diary

of

Signal Squadron, 1st Indian Cavalry Division.

FROM 1st January 1916 TO 31st January 1916.

WAR DIARY or INTELLIGENCE SUMMARY

Army Form C. 2118

Place	Date	Hour	Summary of Events and Information	Remarks and references to Appendices
DARGNIES	1-25 Jany		In billets - Communication with all units. Officers course of instruction (1 hr/hr/hr/hr) on air line was laid 3½ miles from to an E of RESSENVILLE mun ABBEVILLE - DARGNIES going S of FRESSENVILLE & WOINCOURT, then avoiding Power lines & Engineers Road Canadian Cavy Bde.	
to	26/1/16			
to	27/1/16		arrived at FRIVILLE & overhauling receipts night 26/27 Jany. Telegraph communication opened with them at 11 am 27 inst Class of instruction for 6 n.c.o. (Bricks) from units taking place today.	
to	28/1/16			
to	29-31 Jany		In billets. Averagedaily message for week 305.	

P.M. Mannirfalt Capty
1st ?C?

SERIAL NO. 145.

Confidential

War Diary

of

Signal Squadron, 1st Indian Cavalry Division

FROM 1st February 1918 TO 29th February 1918

WAR DIARY
or
INTELLIGENCE SUMMARY
(Erase heading not required.)

Army Form C. 2118

Feby/16.

Place	Date	Hour	Summary of Events and Information	Remarks and references to Appendices
DARGNIES	1 – 13		Billets clean. Officers NCOs under instruction	
	14th		OC RHA moved from BEAUCHAMPS to OFFEUX. Air line to BEAUCHAMPS picked up	
	15th		Air line laid to OC RHA from PEA. Cme at 4PM	
	19th		Brigade line from VALINES to ROGEANREAUL	
	20 – 29		Billets clean. Officers NCOs under instruction. Average number of messages sent by for month 399	

R.W. Hammersburst
Capt
Signals 1st ?

SERIAL NO. 145.

Confidential

War Diary

of

Signal Squadron, 1st Indian Cavalry Division.

FROM 1st March 1916 TO 31st March 1916.

WAR DIARY or INTELLIGENCE SUMMARY

Army Form C. 2118

March 1916.

Place	Date	Hour	Summary of Events and Information	Remarks and references to Appendices
DARGNIES.	23		Orders received that 1st & 9th Coys to start work with III Army future - the 1 & 9 C. H.Q. Coys have been advised. N.C.O.'s & men detailed not to go. They were returned to their units the afternoon. All Sundays on Coy parts. Telegraphic communication cut off with Fred Sqdn " " R.H.Q. & Rocket B.S.	
	24			
	26		" " " DARGNIES to WAIL	
	27		Divisional Report centre moved from DARGNIES to communication re-established by telephone with Rocket B.S. Lloose lines L.G.&.Q. Ypres, G.O.C. Line party out tentatively to LUCKNOW Bde- Mournes party 23 January airline to LUCKNOW Bde.	
	28		Telephone - 2 marches - Communication arranged temporarily with supply chn. 3rd Army school. Rocket Hoo. Field Sqdn Krupp 3rd Army.	
	30		Mr Krupp 3rd Army. Telephone Telephone communication handed out Lucknow Bde & Telephone communication general Rifle B.S.by refurbishing-	
	31		Telephone B.S. Telephone communication cum airline 40 & with aeroplane Spressetz	

SERIAL NO. 145.

Confidential

Cavalry Diary

of

Signal Squadron, 1st Indian Cavalry Division.

FROM 1st April 1916 TO 30th April 1916.

WAR DIARY or INTELLIGENCE SUMMARY

Army Form C. 2118

April 1916.

Place	Date	Hour	Summary of Events and Information	Remarks and references to Appendices
WAIL	1/4/16		Line laid from LUCKNOW Bde to Field Sqdn.	
	6/4/16		Line laid to RQZ Bde	
	7/4/16		Line from N.Z. to get to treatment B.W. exposed - Shrapnel recable replaced by aerial	
	10/4/16		Line laid from CIH to YPRENCH (having come to connect from JHS Gns. both Bde Report centre	
	15/4/16		Advanced report centre spent at YPRENCH for army line between 2 wat HQ working everywhere so	
	29/4/16		Line laid from Lucknow Bde Sqdn.	
	22/4/16		built line from new wait to YPRENCH. Divisle HQ Gns moved Scotes & Mews Bde.	
	23/4/16		Communication restored with Scotes & Mews Bde.	

Daily average number messages 414

R.M. Wainwright
Capt & O.C.
1st Section

SERIAL NO. 14.5.

Confidential

War Diary

of

Signal Squadron, 1st Indian Cavalry Division.

FROM 1st May 1916 TO 30th June 1916.

WAR DIARY or INTELLIGENCE SUMMARY

Army Form C. 2118

May 1916

Place	Date	Hour	Summary of Events and Information	Remarks and references to Appendices
YPRENCH WM6	1-6		In this area for divisional Training	
	7		Returned here today and lives which had previously been.	
LE CAUROY	10		Here today took overians from 6th Corps & 23 divs. moved out in 8th SAN communication at mess with C.A.R. F Co. P.I.B. P.I.E. P.I.H. Reichies.	
	11		Telephone communication established. HQrs Bde 10 Sqn, Field Sqn, BC ase, G & Q Messes, OC supply Col.	
	27		Part of Signal School moved from VACQUERIETTE to GINENCHY LE NOBLE and Telephone communication established with them. Army messages for month of May 409.	
			Enemy average	

R.N. Hammersly Hunt
Capt Signals
1st Ind Canadian

WAR DIARY
or
INTELLIGENCE SUMMARY

(Erase heading not required.)

Army Form C. 2118

June 1916

Place	Date	Hour	Summary of Events and Information	Remarks and references to Appendices
LECROSY	1-29		Nil Beech.	
	30		Mons Li DOUSSENS communication came day with aeeBors PMa c.s.c Staff Messrs Average daily messages for month 423	

R.M.Dawen cright
Capt Sigs
1st Indn Division

SERIAL NO. 145.

Confidential
War Diary
of

Signal Squadron, 1st Indian Cavalry Division.

FROM 1st July 1916 TO 31st July 1916.

Army Form C. 2118

SIGNAL SQUADRON,
1st INDIAN
CAVALRY DIVISION.
No. 149-365/1
Date 1-8-16

WAR DIARY
or
INTELLIGENCE SUMMARY
(Erase heading not required.)

Instructions regarding War Diaries and Intelligence Summaries are contained in F.S. Regs, Part II. and the Staff Manual respectively. Title Pages will be prepared in manuscript.

Place	Date	Hour	Summary of Events and Information	Remarks and references to Appendices
DOULLENS Gnd Achekt	2.7.16 3.7.16		Ordered to proceed to Aune Le Chateau for in communication with 9th army through civil exchange. Obtained my wherewp a line from Aure to P.I.H. (Siedou le fais). Lewis Spiers repaired a line running in W.P.1B (Remainder). R.H.A Bde overhead wires on this line.	
	5.7.16		Line laid W.P.1E (maignevil) no regtl lines are at present bought out to S.Stn. reports that main Amiens line from Aure to Doullens cut several times received orders that it has been cut this afternoon. Send out Cpl Boyce with 2 men. Line was cut at X roads presumably taken it towards LE MÉILLARD. Cpl. Boyce reports front wires.	
	8.7.16		Luneman from CMR arrived with interview wire to put. Line gives ending. It is said that 16th Hr are out and that Doullens line has been cut and went 3 days ago. The Aure - Doullens line which reports wires in presumably refers to this report.	
	10.7.16			
	12.7.16		8th hr receives orders that he has had much correspondence with BSOS states that there has been that their wires is our enemy	

Army Form C. 2118

SIGNAL SQUADRON,
1st INDIAN
CAVALRY DIVISION.
No. HS-86
Date 1-5-16

WAR DIARY or INTELLIGENCE SUMMARY
(Erase heading not required.)

Instructions regarding War Diaries and Intelligence Summaries are contained in F.S. Regs., Part II. and the Staff Manual respectively. Title Pages will be prepared in manuscript.

Place	Date	Hour	Summary of Events and Information	Remarks and references to Appendices
	13		to P.I.B. J.P.I.H. no have Sappers laying a new line & then if poss collect wire left in YPRUCH. Isabell then put up by me in Morn. Pichot Lichour JPKOB at line & movements & wireman Lieutre Lucolhor week in that. Built a divisional Pichot station. Aux le chateau 10 AM opened at VILLERS CHATEL. Closed Ypres at Aux le chateau 10 AM. wk. 3rd Army. 17th Same hour. Telegraphic communicain with Indian Divrs. Corps (Direct). Telephone communication with Indian Divers. BOS.	
VILLERS CHATEL	19.		Telegraphic communication with Secheeb Bde 20th Indrs Lucknow Bde 21st. also 29 Lancers & K. & 9DG through an Exchange. RKA Bde Telephone communication direct. Communications now	
	22		N Drs 22d complete.	
	31		Lucknow Bde moves to CHELERS. SO report cable closed 10 AM. next report cause opens same hour. So see return on new H hand Bde. Sewi. Schenines B2. from H hand Bde. Sewi. Schenines B2. Daily Average of messages for Aug 413	

R. H. Hammersley
Capt OC Sqn

SERIAL No. 145.

Confidential
War Diary
of

Signal Squadron, 1st Indian Cavalry Division.

FROM 1st August 1916 TO 31st August 1916.

Army Form C. 2118

Secret

WAR DIARY
or
INTELLIGENCE SUMMARY

1st Army Signal Squadron 1st August 1916 to 31st August 1916

1st Indian Cavalry Division

Place	Date	Hour	Summary of Events and Information	Remarks and references to Appendices
VILLERS CHATEL	9.8.16 10.8.16		1st Indian Cav Bde moved to VII Corps area - line MILLS Planchong where Bde change billets. HQ Sqn (now consisting three lt C MABLIGNEM previously) was by R.D.G.dn. Hour Order Bde me OKh pain to TINQUES and a rough course on line from there to PERNIN for 6th Dragoons - working supply eln in East return draw an engin to plain SQRS letter for unit & Mhurs Adr between in TINQUES area until moves return wrs Train of Motor cyclists & was having 3 jack with Ban to main Bdr & meet must Soon to 17th Corps North took the pair lines C24 c/5 between VILLERS early to CUMTEL + ROLLECOURT Gave yet supply e lm through PERLETTE . Army Siege Park. Had to take Munakeeng jamspame Mile line	
"	12.8.16		Serving	
"	13.8.16 to 31.8.16		nothing of note . Weekly member Messages forwarded 13084 Daily average 422	

R M Hammersley hust
Capt Cmdg Signal CSqdn 1st Indian Cav Div

SERIAL NO. 145.

Confidential
War Diary
of

Signal Squadron, 1st Indian Cavalry Division.

FROM 1st September 1916 TO 30th September 1916.

WAR DIARY or INTELLIGENCE SUMMARY

Army Form C. 2118

CAVALRY DIVISION
No. HS-74D
Date 1-18-16

September 1916
1st Indian Cavalry Bde.

Place	Date	Hour	Summary of Events and Information	Remarks and references to Appendices
FROHEN LE GRAND	2.9.16		Divnl. H.Qrs. moved from VILLERS CHATEL today report came therewith at 10 am. Wireless section was taken away. Day evening from WARLUS where it had been set up to arrange to ask wireless 111 Army Corps Sinceling Normal personnel for a task.	
	3.9.16		Report centre moves LST RIQUIER opening there 11 am 3.9.16 in communication with keepers of Phot & ace some units at once - line to be knocked to Lieprond B.G. Buct line to Lieprond B.Gr. at B.ARNIEY - a reference from below at NOYELLE EN CHAUSSEE.	
	4.9.16		Report centre ST RIQUIER closed 11 am opens) DOULLENS same hour. In communication unit forwarding drink units. 3 B.des. RHA, B.Gr. Raiders (Bousmanson) C.A.S.E.	
DOULLENS	11.9.16		Report centre closes Doullens 12 noon opens MEZONNELE same hour.	
MEZONVILLE	13.9.16		Report centre closed MEZONVILLE 9 am 13/9/16 on (phone) We opened at MOREAUCOURT at time activities was w3 Corps w3 telephoned at exchange. I showed 9 am communication through 14 Corps w/t Advanced Cavy. Corps. Direct line verified, found but it was not in pain nor incorrect number given for through by morse telephone at 3 pm at 11.30 respectively.	
MOREANCOURT	15/9/16		M.D.A.T at 10 a.m.	

WAR DIARY
or
INTELLIGENCE SUMMARY

Army Form C. 2118

Place	Date	Hour	Summary of Events and Information	Remarks and references to Appendices
MORLANCOURT	15/9/16		Arranged for an officer of RFC to lecture all Signalling officers of the Division on procedure when working with aeroplanes and rowing open front trench.	
"	18/9/16		2RC lent over to all Brigades	
"	19/9/16		Brevet Lieut Col GS very unsatisfactory working with 2RC never arrived here, has written a very unsatisfactory working with 2RC. coy corps. He first said it was manned by X Corps. Spoke to GSAS Corps coy corps. He maintains is himself. My opinion is he has no turn out half nights night set a fair p/u off	
"	23/9/16		are frequently not truthful. MONTAUBAN 10 am. & VIA at FRICOURT 10 am. P1H V2R opened as MONTAUBAN 10 am. & MORLANCOURT line.	
MONTAUBAN	25/9/16		line was 2RC – MORLANCOURT NDNS on 23/9/16 was not connected up. The arrangements made with NDNS on 23/9/16 was not connected up. Effect – 9 took action at once is upon an answer. About 2.30 pm 3 got GS team to GS coy corps, was in every hut through at 3.30 pm. She was a great confusion upper there over things sent with respect that Staff Cassis up/r their over things sent to VIA. sent with summons of information even sent to VIA. Switch – asked for at MONTAUBAN 10.30 am. did not arrive till 12.25pm. They were first sent to FRICOURT arriving than 12 morn. Wires received from coy corps today – horses very poor condition – as MORLANCOURT 9 pm. V2R etc.	

Signed Captain General

WAR DIARY
or
INTELLIGENCE SUMMARY

Army Form C. 2118

(Erase heading not required.)

Place	Date	Hour	Summary of Events and Information	Remarks and references to Appendices
MORLANCOURT	25/9/16		MONTAUBAN 8 pm. Jones at FRICOURT 7.30 pm	
"	26/9/16		ADMS Corps Cavy wires that James at ZRE - VIA had been in VIA Office late he felt it extreme from permanent hold to our officer. Sent after Sherman out to carry out the Cumcally discussed 26XIV Corps was lead in – on the depots	
BOSSY LES DAOURS	27/9/16		Report centre closes MORLANCOURT 3 pm. Opens at BOSSY LES DAOURS. Same had 16 Z Co functions were completed about 10.30 pm for things about 12.20 am. Bus is moving by enemy. apen Report centre closes BOSSY LES DAOURS 10 am. Opens PICQUIGNY 10 am. to PIBEPIE	
PICQUIGNY	28/9/16		Somewhat. Telephone communication was Opened at MILLY. Point Report centre closes PICQUIGNY 10 am. made arrangements with X Corps hour. On telephone Greek Boos. any officer for three lines – which he had did with 10 am + 9 pm in LIGESCOURT Some home, but manage to Z co line and long through all offices. Report centre as opened to centre as only code had along same home - Which was answers from Rear report centre at time when 9 am at MILLY at 11.10 am -	
MILLY LE HAUT CLOCHER	29/9/16			
LIGESCOURT	30/9/16		the Ground – direct line was cut. General permanent line of 0.35 pm through by 11 am has cut	

WAR DIARY
or
INTELLIGENCE SUMMARY

(Erase heading not required.)

Army Form C. 2118

Place	Date	Hour	Summary of Events and Information	Remarks and references to Appendices

found onto it. Mr Mes reports.
Report received from R.A.F. Corps Cmdrs that communic a time
on the previous on 23/9/16 were unsatisfactory. Efforts up to
report to my G.S. showing the difficulties has been worked
under came to some when Cavy Corps signals

War messages for month 13627
4514
barely average.

R Manners Coy hunt
Capt
Signals Sqdn
Commdg 1st Bds.

SERIAL NO. 145.

Confidential
War Diary
of

Signal Squadron, 4th Cavalry Division. (late 1st Ind. Cavy. Divn).

FROM 1st October 1916 TO 31st October 1916.
30th November 1916.

WAR DIARY or INTELLIGENCE SUMMARY

Army Form C. 2118

1st October 1916

Place	Date	Hour	Summary of Events and Information	Remarks and references to Appendices
16E SCOOP	1/10/16		Asked Corr Corps if they could furnish any G.S. wire Relay twins to Bdes. NSNS replies in negative & code this is prohibited by OB. Have referred matter to Army G.S. who sans wire code arrived no put answer were WP1H army phones trumps peb arrived.	
"	2/10/16		polar motor returned from BIZZON Farm yesterday horses are wireless motion returned have reported matter to General Staff in disgraceful condition.	
"	3/10/16		(poles code 57) WMhonBde at DOURIEZ was Buck line — VIRONCHUR for schemes tactical line to VIRONCHUR for schemes G.OC and NFOS inspired Monsieur Tofe about Bde busenced 3 resting. Continued RHA Bde brick line (code D3) to Durat HdQrs not got through. Peachet Bde. Arranged with Sigs Peachet complete line to leave our exchange when out + use for Bde for them.	
"	5/10/16		Commence a try through Bde rehearsal of Cavy dash in 25/9/16 carried out Schaemsfelt Hous lines branch smoothly Technical communications seemed...	
"	6/10/16		no hitches but MhonBde Signals were informed that Army Phones not use M/E OPs as not we are made practical.	

WAR DIARY
INTELLIGENCE SUMMARY

Army Form C. 2118

October 1916

Place	Date	Hour	Summary of Events and Information	Remarks and references to Appendices
LIGESCOURT	9/10/16		Capt. A.H.A. Emperor, 8th Cavalry, took over command of Squadron	
	11-10-16 16/10/16		Communication to holes by wire, & 2 C.O. and staff officers by wire.	
	20th		Wireless moved to Cav. Corps? Wire for use in next area. Indented to 40 miles G.I. wire. No G.I. wire. Advance party proceeded to ST. VALERY to start building line. No G.I. wire received.	
	31st		Began laying enamelled wire in new area, as no G.I. wire had arrived.	

W.M.Simpson Capt
Signal Squadron.
1st Ind. Cav. Div.

Army Form C. 2118

ON 627

WAR DIARY or INTELLIGENCE SUMMARY

SIGNAL SQUADRON 1st I.C.D. NOVEMBER 1916

(Erase heading not required.)

Instructions regarding War Diaries and Intelligence Summaries are contained in F.S. Regs., Part II. and the Staff Manual respectively. Title Pages will be prepared in manuscript.

Place	Date	Hour	Summary of Events and Information	Remarks and references to Appendices
LIGESCOURT	1st		VZR opened at ST. VALERY at 10AM working to ABBEVILLE PIE closed DOURIEZ 8.0AM. Line to them at ESCARBOTIN completed at 2 PM.	
	2nd	11.30AM	VIA closed LIGESCOURT and reopened ST VALERY	
			Cine. open by phone to PIB and Civil ST VALERY	
		5 PM	Phone to G.O.C. " " " Q	
		6 PM	" " Field Squadron. " " " G	
	3rd		Line laid to ASC	
			Line party out on lines to Lucknow Bde and Supply Clm.	
	4th	1 PM	Cine with Supply Column	
	5th		much trouble with line to ABBEYILLE	
	6th	9.15AM	Phone to PIH 9-15AM through PIE	
		9-35AM	ABBEVILLE line faulty	
		10-15AM	Field Squadron line broken - repaired 11-30AM	
	7th	12.25PM	Heavy wind. AB line broken.	
		2.30PM	AB line repaired.	
	8th		Routine work	
	9th		Routine work. 8 officers joined for Class. Lt BOYD 17th Lancers attached as Instructor	
	10th		ABBEVILLE line faulty	

Army Form C. 2118

WAR DIARY
or
INTELLIGENCE SUMMARY

(Erase heading not required.)

Signal September 1st I. C. D.

Place	Date	Hour	Summary of Events and Information	Remarks and references to Appendices
ST VALERY	11th		Line party for Cavalry Corps working on line to Brigades. Telephone to Civil School through Civil	
	12th		Routine work	
	13th		Routine work	
	14th	10.45 AM	AB line faults. Intermittent faults all day owing to working parties	
	15th	11 AM	Through to PLH via AB. Double current working.	
	16th	11.35 AM	AB line faults	
		12.11 PM	Fault cleared	
		3.30 PM	AB line faulty till 4 PM	
	17th		Continued trouble with AB line till 11 AM.	
	18th	8.30 AM	Direct working to 2 C.O. AB intermediate	
	19th		routine work	
	20th		ditto	
	21st		Semi-permanent lines completed and S.C. working begun to P13 and P1E. Line parties on trouble	
			to RTO camp A.H.T. Coy.	
	22nd		Telephone to A.H.T. Coy and Rilheem	
	23rd		Routine work	
	24th	4.45 PM	P1E line down. Break repaired 8.30 pm.	
	25th		Routine working	
	26th		AB line faulty. Linemen found ir clear to SAIGNEVILLE. AB linemen cleared fault 4 PM	
			Lt. E.N.W. JOHNSTON required 24th Lancers	

A.S. Simpson Capt.
4th Division Signal Squadron

WAR DIARY or INTELLIGENCE SUMMARY

(Erase heading not required.)

4th Cav. Divl Signal Squadron 2 NOVEMBER

Army Form C. 2118

Place	Date	Hour	Summary of Events and Information	Remarks and references to Appendices
ST. VALERY	27/4/16		Title of Squadron changed to 4th Divl. Signal Squadron	
	28th		AB line faulty 10-30 AM — 10-45 AM.	
			AB line faults at intervals throughout the day	
	29th		Routine work	
	30th		AB line continually faulty — All these faults have been at AT3 end.	
			Total mss. for month 17225	
			Maximum 710	
			Minimum 354	

A.W. Thompson Lt/Mr
4th Divl Signal Squadron

SERIAL NO. 145.

Confidential
War Diary
of

Signal Squadron, 4th Cavalry Division.

FROM 1st December 1916 TO 31st December 1916.

WAR DIARY or INTELLIGENCE SUMMARY

Signal Squadron 4th Cav. Div.

DECEMBER 1916

Place	Date	Hour	Summary of Events and Information	Remarks and references to Appendices
ST VALERY	1/12/16		Communications as in diagram attached (App. A)	
	2nd		Trouble with AB line	
	3rd		Routine	
	4th 5th 6th		Routine	
	7th		"	
	8th		AB line faulty. Direct Cmn with 2CO	
			2CO line giving trouble	
	9th		Routine	
	10th		"	
	11th		"	
	12th		2CO line fell down between canal ST VALERY & NOYELLES – cleared 8 pm	
	13th		routine	
	14th		2CO line faulty 11-55. Pull breaks 2-30 pm – cleared 3-30 pm	
	15-28th		routine – Communication also satisfactory	
	29th		PH line faulty – pole down 1 mile E of BOISMONT	
	30-31st		Routine – Communications still as in diagram. Total rain for month 17141	Maximum 651 Minimum 366

Communications VD

12.12.16 2nd Anzac Corps.

Appendix "A"

1 IND CAV DIV. TROOPS.

1 INDIAN ROYAL HORSE ARTILLERY
1914 SEPT TO 1916 DEC

ROUSE'S BRIGADE R.H.A.
1914 SEPT TO 1914 NOV.

DIV AMMN COLUMN R.H.A.
1914 AUG TO 1916 DEC,

1 INDIAN FIELD SQUADRON
ROYAL ENGINEERS.
1915 FEB TO 1916 DEC.

2 FIELD TROOP SAPPERS & MINERS.
1914 SEPT TO 1915 NOV.

DIV SIGNAL SQUADRON
1914 DEC TO 1916 DEC.

117D

1 IND CAV DIV. TROOPS.

1 INDIAN ROYAL HORSE ARTILLERY
1914 SEPT TO 1916 DEC.

ROUSE'S BRIGADE R.H.A.
1914 SEPT TO 1914 NOV.

DIV AMMN COLUMN R.H.A.
1914 AUG TO 1916 DEC,

1 INDIAN FIELD SQUADRON ROYAL ENGINEERS.
1915 FEB TO 1916 DEC.

2 FIELD TROOP SAPPERS & MINERS.
1914 SEPT TO 1915 NOV.

DIV SIGNAL SQUADRON
1914 DEC TO 1916 DEC.

1170

WAR DIARY

OF

H.Q.rs R.A

1st INDIAN CAVALRY DIVISION

MARCH - 1915.

WAR DIARY

OF

H^DQ^{RS} R A

1ST INDIAN CAVALRY DIVISION

FEBRUARY - 1915

www.ingramcontent.com/pod-product-compliance
Lightning Source LLC
Chambersburg PA
CBHW081241170426
43191CB00034B/2007